You're the Actual Best

WRITTEN BY M. H. Clark
ILLUSTRATED BY Chloe Welch

I've thought this for a while,
and I finally ran some tests.
It's just as I suspected...

You're the *actual* best.

For starters, your heart's a bit bigger than most.
It's how you care so hugely and so deeply.

And it's why,
when you show up for people,
you show up so completely.

You've got the perfect blend
of silliness and seriousness.

(A difficult balance to strike, but somehow you do it.)

And there's something about the way you're you
that makes me feel good being me.

I don't even think you have to try.
It happens so effortlessly.

With you, all the great days
are always more great.
But the bad days are better too.

It's your words and your kindness...
but while that's all true,

it's mostly your presence.
The fact is: it's you.

In all the time I've known you,
you only get better and better.
And just when I think
you've reached the limit...

You surpass it.

See, the World's Best Person Graph
just doesn't lie.
Oops... it looks like the numbers
don't quite go that high.

NOTES

Which just means, of course,
that you're way off the charts.

(For the record, I knew you'd be,
right from the start.)

So thank goodness you're here.

Thank goodness you're <u>you</u>.

And thank goodness for
all of the good things you do.

Thank goodness you're wildly one of a kind.
One hundred and sixteen percent of the time.

Because people like you make this world go round.

But people like you aren't that easily found.

I don't have the numbers
or figures quite yet.
But I *can* tell you this:
you're as rare as it gets.

And now that I know
you're the actual best,
I realize that makes me...
the luckiest.

But I don't need statistics
or science or proof
to show me that this is
the actual truth.

What makes me more lucky
than anyone else?

You do, every day,
just by being yourself.

COMPENDIUM®
live inspired

Written by: M.H. Clark
Illustrated by: Chloe Welch
Edited by: Amelia Riedler
Art Direction by: Chelsea Bianchini

ISBN: 978-1-957891-35-4

1st printing. Printed in China with soy inks on FSC®-Mix certified paper.

Create meaningful moments with gifts that inspire.

CONNECT WITH US
live-inspired.com | sayhello@compendiuminc.com

@compendiumliveinspired
#compendiumliveinspired